Getting Ready

A Career as a Computer Technician

by Bill Lund

Content Consultant:
James W. Cortada
IBM Consulting Group
IBM Corporation

CAPSTONE PRESS

MANKATO, MINNESOTA

C A P S T O N E P R E S S

818 North Willow Street • Mankato, Minnesota 56001
http://www.capstone-press.com

Printed in the United States of America.

Library of Congress Cataloging-in-Publication Data
Lund, Bill, 1954-
    Getting ready for a career as a computer technician
    p. cm.
    Includes bibliographical references and index.
    Summary: Provides an overview of the work done by the technicians who
install and maintain computer equipment and systems and briefly describes
career opportunities in the field.
    ISBN 1-56065-550-X
    1. Computers--Maintenance and repair--Juvenile literature.
    2. Electronic technicians--Vocational guidance--Juvenile literature.
[1. Computers--Maintenance and repair--Vocational guidance. 2. Vocational
guidance.] I. Title.
TK7887.L86   1998
621.39'16--dc21

                                                97-12209
                                                   CIP
                                                   AC

Photo credits
FPG, 37; Ron Routar, 4; Reggie Parker, 7, Stephen Simpson, 8,
    30, 34, 43; Tom Wilson, 10; Telegraph Colour Library 12, 26;
    T. Tracy, 15; Jeff Kaufman, 18, 28; Donal Philby, 22;
    Court Mast, 25; Robert Keeling, 38; Richard Gaul, 44;
    Carl Vanderschvit, 47
Unicorn Stock, 16; R.J. Production, cover; Robert Cristian, 20;
    Wayne Floyd, 32

Table of Contents

Chapter One
Working With Computers

Today, almost everyone uses computers.
People use computers in school, at work, and
at home. Even people who do not own
computers use computers almost every day.
Video games are computers. Calculators are
small computers that do math. Even televisions
and videocasette recorders have computers
in them.

Most computers are connected to
peripherals. A peripheral is a device such as a
printer that is connected to a computer. A
computer cannot do its job without its

Today, almost everyone uses computers.

peripherals. Other peripherals include modems, disk drives, and monitors.

A modem is a device used to send information between computers through telephone lines. A disk drive is the part of the computer that reads information from a diskette. It can also store information on a diskette. A monitor is the computer's display screen.

Computers and peripherals are machines. Machines break down. A computer technician is called to fix them when they do.

Computer Technicians

A computer technician is a person who keeps computers working. Technicians set computers up, maintain them, and repair them.

There are many kinds of computers. Each has different uses. Computers must be set up, maintained, and fixed in a variety of ways. There are many kinds of computer technicians to fix different computers.

Computer technicians set computers up, maintain them, and repair them.

Computer technicians work in many areas.

Computer technicians work in many areas. Some fix personal computers. A personal computer is a computer used by a single person or family. Some fix peripherals. Other computer technicians fix servers and very large computers. A server is a large and powerful computer that connects other computers in a network. A network is a group of computers that are connected to each other. Networks allow people to share information. The Internet is one very big network.

Where Technicians Work

Many computer technicians work for companies whose business is fixing other people's computers. They travel to schools, offices, and businesses to fix broken computers.

Other computer technicians work for businesses that use computers. The computer technician is an important part of the company. Some of these businesses have thousands of computers and peripherals. Often, these businesses use computers all day and all night. If the computers break down, people cannot do their work. Full-time technicians keep everything working.

Some computer technicians work for companies that make or sell computers. The companies give warranties on their computers. A warranty is a written promise to fix something. The companies promise to send computer technicians to fix computers that break down.

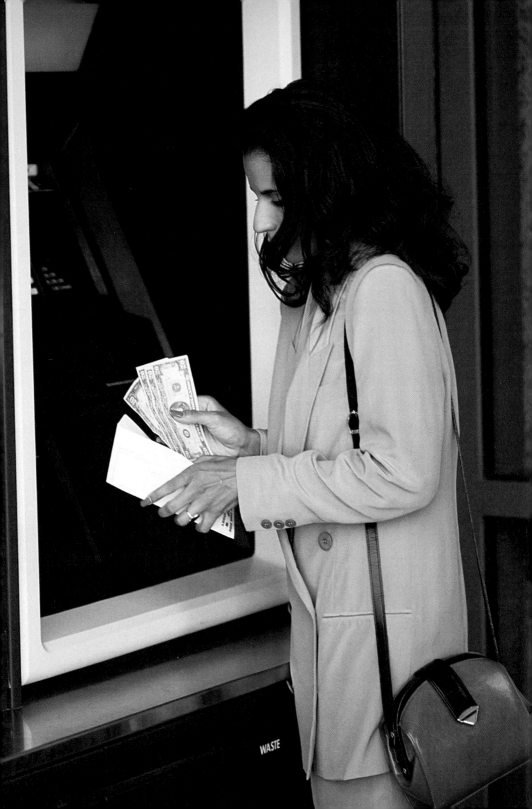

Other computer technicians are self-employed. Self-employed means they own their own businesses. Self-employed technicians work for other companies through contracts. A contract is a written agreement to work on a project. When a project is done, self-employed technicians go to work for another company.

Computers Are Everywhere

There are many computer technicians who do not work on personal computers or servers. They work on computers found in other machines. Some work on arcade games. Others work on computers inside car engines or video cameras. There are computers in airplanes, grocery stores, banks, and countless other places. When they break down, computer technicians must repair them.

There are computers almost everywhere, including banks.

PROBE TRONICS INC.   MODEL
                                      REV D 10-701-6
                             TELTEC 01V 2389

Chapter 2
Important Skills

All technicians share a number of skills. They work well with their hands. They have good vision. They are good at solving problems. Most important, they must speak clearly and listen closely to understand the problem.

Manual Dexterity and Vision
Manual dexterity is one of the most important skills for computer technicians. Manual dexterity is the ability to work well with the hands.

Computer technicians must work well with their hands.

Technicians use many small tools when they fix computers. Technicians need to have good manual dexterity because many computer parts are small and fragile.

Technicians also need good vision. Small computer parts can be hard to see. Many of the wires in a computer have special colors. The color of a wire tells technicians what the wire does. Computer technicians have to know what each color means.

Problem Solving

Another important skill for computer technicians is problem solving. Technicians must be able to figure out why computers break down. They have to think clearly.

Fixing a computer can be like solving a mystery. Technicians are like detectives. They find clues and then figure out what is wrong. This is called troubleshooting.

Many computer parts are small and fragile.

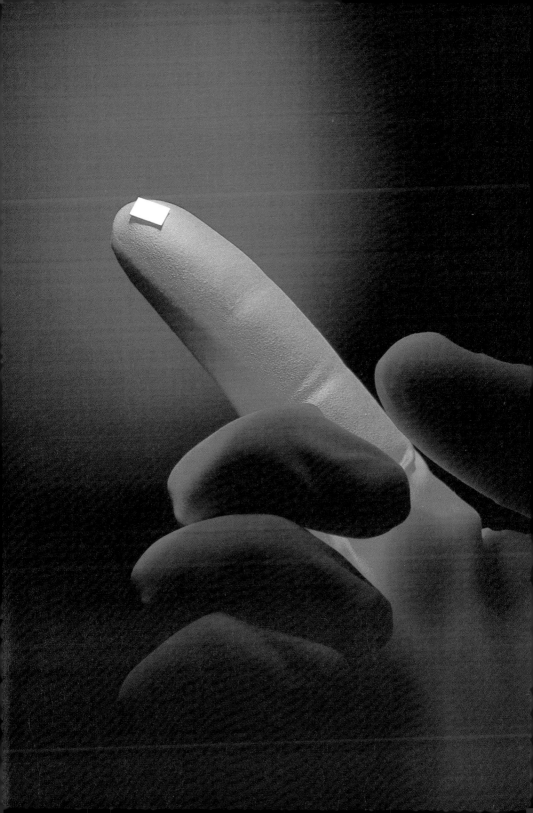

Communication Skills

Computer technicians speak and listen well. This is called communication. Strong communication skills help technicians understand the needs of their customers. Sometimes, customers can tell a technician what the problem is. This cuts down on troubleshooting time.

Computer technicians often go to places they have never been before. They talk to the people that own broken computers. They ask questions about how each computer broke down and about which parts do not work. They must listen carefully, so they know what is wrong.

People need to know why their computers break. Technicians also have to explain what is wrong with broken computers. This can be difficult. Many people do not understand how computers work. Technicians have to use words and ideas that people understand. Technicians can prevent some problems

Technicians have to explain what is wrong with broken computers.

from happening again by explaining what went wrong.

Sometimes people become angry when their computers do not work properly. A computer technician must be patient and understanding. It is important that computer technicians are friendly. The technician is sometimes blamed when the computer breaks. Sometimes people forget that computers are just machines.

Computer technicians have good communication skills.

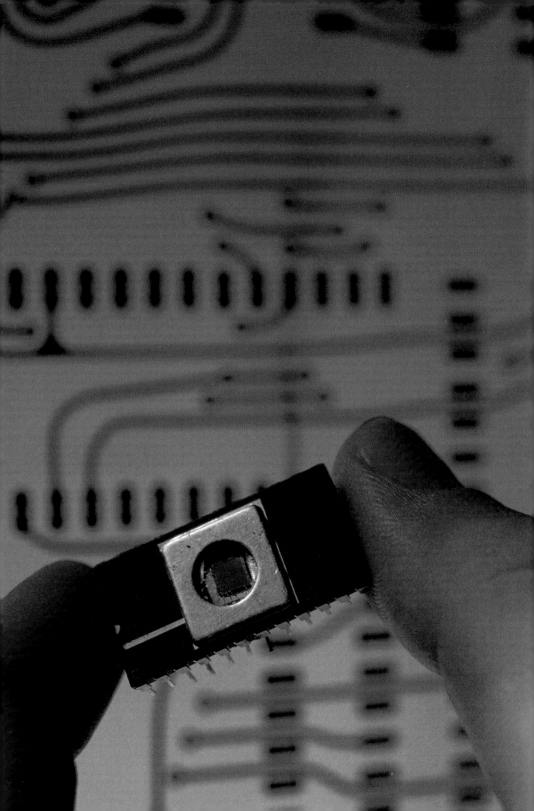

Chapter 3

A Technician's Tasks

Some computer technicians help install computers. Install means to set up a computer. These technicians also get the computers ready to work. The technicians lay the cables that connect the computers to their peripherals. They set up networks and make sure everything is connected properly. Once everything is ready, the technicians test the computers to make sure everything works.

Many technicians also maintain the computers they install. They take care of all the parts. They use small tools to clean and adjust the parts. This way, small problems can be fixed before they become big problems.

Computer technicians take care of small parts.

Finding the Problem

Many companies cannot do business without computers. Computer breakdowns can be serious and costly. Computer technicians need to find and solve the problems as quickly as possible.

When computers break, computer technicians must conduct a diagnosis. Diagnose means to find the cause of a problem.

Sometimes, computer technicians use special computer programs to find the problems. A program is a set of coded instructions that tells a computer what to do. The programs used by technicians are called diagnostic programs. Diagnostic programs sometimes tell technicians what is broken.

The diagnostic programs technicians use are like the programs mechanics use to fix cars.

Computer technicians must diagnose problems quickly.

Some diagnostic programs tell technicians exactly how to fix the computers. Many computers can even run diagnostic programs by themselves.

Repairs

Computer technicians fix the problems they diagnose. Some problems are easy to fix. Special computer software can solve these problems. Software is a set of programs that tells a computer what to do.

Other times, computers need new parts. Computer technicians replace broken parts with new ones. Sometimes technicians replace circuit boards. A circuit board is a series of circuits. A circuit is a path for electricity to flow through. Circuit boards control many of the computer's functions. They are among the most important parts of computers.

Circuit boards control many of a computer's functions.

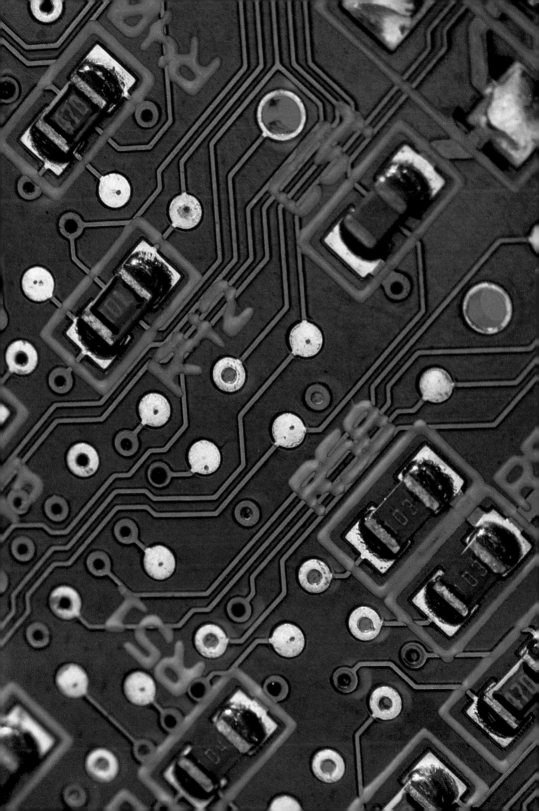

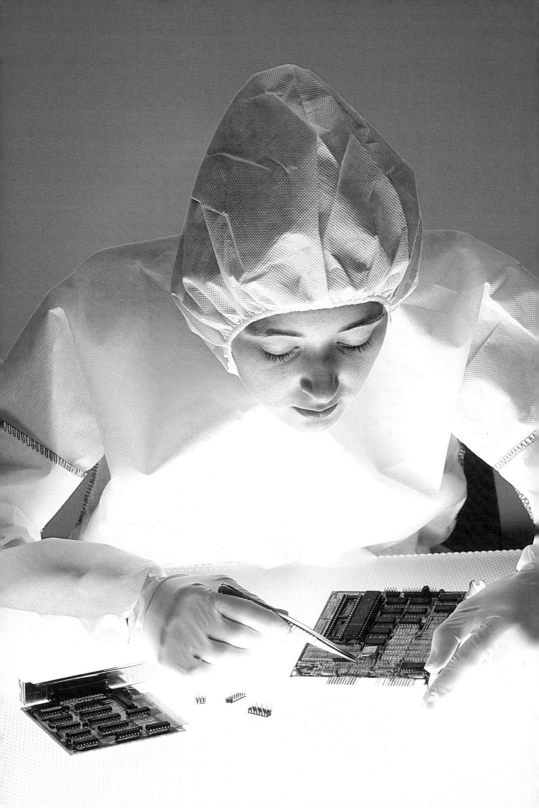

Some problems are not so easy to fix. Technicians might have to take broken computers back to their workshops. Some technicians replace the customers' computers with another computer until repairs are finished. Replacement computers are called loaners. Loaners help companies keep working while technicians repair the broken computers.

Some computer problems are not easy to fix.

Chapter 4

Work Setting

Computer technicians work in all kinds of settings. Many have to go wherever there are problems. They fix computers in offices, stores, and schools. Sometimes technicians travel to different cities.

Some computer technicians work for just one company. They may not have to travel as much. Most of their work is done in one office building.

Computer technicians fix computers in offices, stores, and schools.

Work Day

Many computer technicians work long hours. Some companies use computers 24 hours every day. Technicians must be ready whenever computers or peripherals break down. Often, computer technicians have pagers. A pager is an electronic beeping device that lets people contact technicians. Technicians can be reached even in the middle of the night.

Computer technicians often have to work independently. Usually only one technician works on a problem at a time. Technicians must be able to work without anyone telling them what to do. They need to be able to do their jobs without any guidance.

Technicians must be ready whenever computers or peripherals break down.

Salary

In the late 1990s, most computer technicians earned between $17,000 and $40,000 per year.

Technicians who work with more complex equipment earn more money. Technicians also earn more money based on how many kinds of computers they can fix. Some companies have many kinds of computers.

Sometimes, technicians have to work on holidays. Many also work overtime. Overtime is when people work longer than usual. Usually, technicians are paid more if they work overtime or on holidays.

In the late 1990s, most computer technicians earned between $17,000 and $40,000 per year.

Chapter 4

Training for Tomorrow

Today, there are more computers than ever before. The computers are becoming faster and more complex. Technicians must have education and training.

The first step to becoming a computer technician is finishing high school. High school classes in math, physics, electronics, and computer programming are helpful.

After high school, most computer technicians attend technical schools or junior colleges. Technicians take special classes about computer repair. They learn about electronics, computer languages, and how to use technicians' tools. They also learn about safety.

Classes in math, physics, electronics, and computer programming help future technicians.

Technicians go through one or two years of training before they are ready to work.

Other technicians are trained in the military. People trained in the military receive hands-on training on modern equipment. The military needs good technicians to keep everything from airplanes to radar machines working. A radar machine uses radio waves to locate and guide objects. Demand for technicians trained in the military is high.

Most technicians are not independent on their first jobs. Instead, they work as apprentices. An apprentice is someone who learns by working with a skilled person. Apprentices watch, learn, and help when they can. During this time, they see how experienced technicians handle problems.

Most technicians spend three to six months as apprentices. When they are ready, they work by themselves. If they are good at their jobs, they might train their own apprentices someday.

Some computer technicians are trained in the military.

Keeping Up

Computers keep getting faster and more powerful. Every year, new computers have new features. Technicians must learn about the new computer features. Technicians who do not keep learning have trouble fixing new computers.

Technicians need to understand how the newest computers work. They read manuals to keep up with changes in computers. A manual is a book that tells how to operate or repair something.

Technicians also take classes to learn new skills. They work with the latest computers in these classes. Often, the companies that technicians work for send them to the classes.

The Future of Computers

As computers become more complex, they become harder to fix and understand. There will always be jobs for people who understand and know how to fix computers.

Technicians read manuals to keep up with new computers.

Words to Know

apprentice (uh-PREN-tiss)—someone who learns by working with a skilled person

circuit (SUR-kit)—a path for electricity to flow through

circuit board (SUR-kit BORD)—a series of circuits that controls many of a computer's functions

contract (KON-trakt)—a written agreement to work on a project

diagnose (dye-uhg-NOHSS)—to find the cause of a problem

install (in-STAWL)—to set up computers and get them ready to work

manual (MAN-yoo-uhl)—a book that tells how to operate or repair something

manual dexterity (MAN-yoo-uhl dek-STER-uh-tee)—the ability to work with the hands

network (NET-wurk)—a group of computers connected to each other

peripheral (puh-RIF-ur-uhl)—a device such as a printer that is connected to a computer

personal computer (PUR-suh-nuhl kuhm-PYOO-tur)—a computer used by a single person or family

program (PROH-gram)—coded instructions that tell a computer what to do

server (SUR-vur)—a large and powerful computer that connects other computers in a network

software (SAWFT-wair)—a set of programs that tells a computer what to do

warranty (WOR-uhn-tee)—a written promise to fix something

To Learn More

Eberts, Marjorie. *Computers*. Lincolnwood, Ill.: VGM Career Horizons, 1995.

Lund, Bill. *Getting Ready for a Career as an Internet Designer*. Mankato, Minn.: Capstone Press, 1998.

Kaplan, Andrew. *Careers for Computer Buffs*. Brookfield, Conn.: Millbrook Press, 1991.

Spencer, Jean W. *Careers Inside the World of Technology*. New York: Rosen Publishing Group, 1995.

Weigant, Chris. *Choosing a Career in Computers*. New York: Rosen Publishing Group, 1997.

Computer technicians who work with complex computers usually earn more money.

Useful Addresses

Computer Science Association
Fifth floor
243 College Street
Toronto, Ontario M5Y 2Y1
Canada

Electronics Technicians Association
604 North Jackson
Greencastle, IN 46135

National Association of Trade and Technical Schools
2251 Wisconsin Avenue NW
Washington DC 20007

North American Computer Service Association
506 Georgetown Dr.
Casselberry, FL 32707

The first step to becoming a computer technician is to finish high school.

Internet Sites

JobGuide Online: Computer Service Technician
http://www.edna.edu.au/JobGuideOnline/Text/Jobs/431511A.html

Logo - Computer Programming for Kids
http://www.magma.ca/~dsleeth/kids/lessons

Just for Middle School Kids
http://www.westnet.com/~rickd/Kids.html

A circuit board is a large series of electrical pathways.

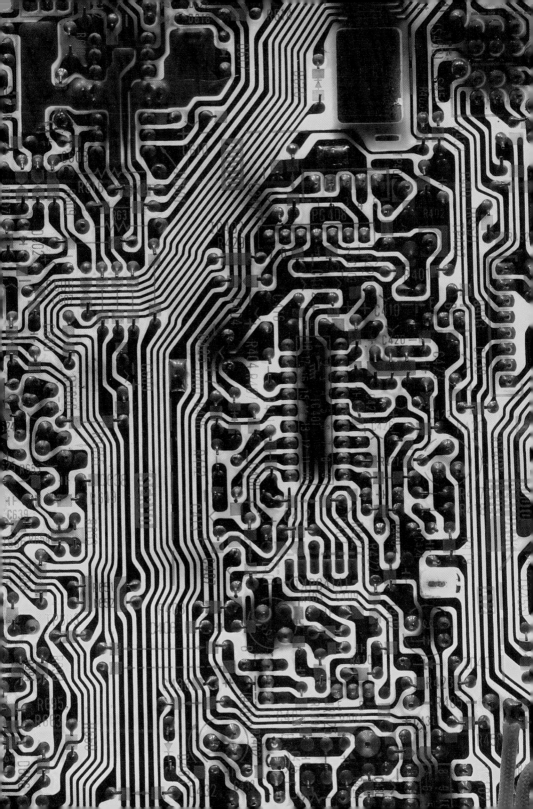

Index